WEIRD FOOD

By Virginia Loh-Hagan

45th Parallel Press

Published in the United States of America by Cherry Lake Publishing
Ann Arbor, Michigan
www.cherrylakepublishing.com

Reading Adviser: Marla Conn MS, Ed., Literacy specialist, Read-Ability, Inc.
Book Designer: Melinda Millward

45th Parallel Press is an imprint of Cherry Lake Publishing.

Library of Congress Cataloging-in-Publication Data

Names: Loh-Hagan, Virginia, author.
Title: Weird food / by Virginia Loh-Hagan.
Description: Ann Arbor : Cherry Lake Publishing, 2017. | Series: Stranger than fiction | Includes bibliographical references and index. | Audience: Grades 4 to 6.
Identifiers: LCCN 2017001049| ISBN 9781634728874 (hardcover) | ISBN 9781634729765 (pdf) | ISBN 9781534100657 (pbk.) | ISBN 9781534101548 (hosted ebook)
Subjects: LCSH: Food—Juvenile literature. | Food habits—Miscellanea—Juvenile literature. | Eccentrics and eccentricities—Juvenile literature.
Classification: LCC TX355 .L66 2017 | DDC 641.3—dc23
LC record available at https://lccn.loc.gov/2017001049

Printed in the United States of America
Corporate Graphics

About the Author

Dr. Virginia Loh-Hagan is an author, university professor, former classroom teacher, and curriculum designer. She loves food. The strangest thing she's ever eaten is snails. She lives in San Diego with her very tall husband and very naughty dogs. To learn more about her, visit www.virginialoh.com.

Table of Contents

Introduction

People eat all kinds of things. They eat to **survive**. Survive means to stay alive. They need food. Food gives them energy. Food builds muscles. Food keeps their organs working. Food keeps them healthy. Food also makes some people happy. They enjoy eating. They try new things. Other people are picky. They're scared of anything different. They'd never eat anything strange.

There's strange food. And then, there's really strange food. Some people eat super strange food. It's so strange that it's hard to believe. It sounds like fiction. But these stories are all true!

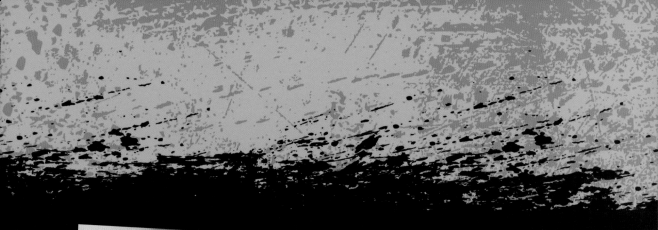

Human bodies are eating machines.

chapter one

Bugs

Two billion people around the world eat bugs. Some people live in warm weather. They're more likely to eat bugs. Bugs like warm weather. Beetles, caterpillars, bees, wasps, and ants are the most popular.

Rose Wang and Laura D'Asaro are Americans. They sell food made from bugs. They grinded roasted crickets. They combined them with bean flour. They made chips. They called them Chirps.

Many people choose to eat bugs. Some Thai people fry scorpions. Some

Some people farm bugs for food.

Mexicans dip locusts in chocolate. Some Chinese boil water bugs. Some Ghanians bake termites into bread.

7

Many people don't choose to eat bugs. But they do. They just don't know it. Americans eat 1 to 2 pounds (0.5 to 1 kilogram) of bugs every year.

A government group is in charge of food safety. It allows bugs in our foods. But there's a rule. Bugs aren't allowed to affect how food looks.

Mites are tiny white bugs. They're in wheat and other grains. They're in frozen vegetables. Fruit flies are in canned fruit. They're in raisins. Bugs are everywhere.

Some experts think eating bugs is healthy.

Explained by Science

Dr. Michael Levitt is a stomach doctor. He smells farts. He sniffs out health problems. Bad farts smell like "rotten eggs." Too much of this smell is unhealthy. It could mean a disease. He worked with 16 healthy people. The people ate beans. He trapped their fart gas. He put it in containers. He collected over 100 samples. Odor testers opened each container. They smelled the fart gas. They judged each smell. Human stomach smells are important. Farts have different smells. They are bitter, savory, sweet, fishy, or meaty. A meaty smell is bad. A fishy smell is bad. Farts are connected to what we eat. Smelling farts is a science!

chapter two

Dirt

Some people eat dirt. They eat it raw. They cook it. They bake it. Sera Young is an **expert**. She studies eating dirt. She said Native Americans ate dirt.

Kaolin is white dirt. It's soft clay. It's chalky. It's used to make paper and paint. Some **pregnant** women crave kaolin. Pregnant means they're carrying a baby. They may feel sick. They may feel like throwing up. Eating clay makes them feel better. Clay absorbs things. It draws out bad things. Some think clay can get rid of poisons.

Children often eat dirt.

chapter three

Moving Octopus

Japanese and Koreans eat *odori don*. This is a special dish. It's an octopus. The brain is removed. The octopus is dead. But it's fresh. It's placed on a dish.

People pour soy sauce on it. The octopus moves. It flaps its **tentacles**. Tentacles are limbs. It looks like it's escaping. The octopus still has nerves. Soy sauce has salt. The salt triggers the octopus.

The dish doesn't taste like anything. But that's not why people eat it. Tentacles move in people's mouths. People like how this

People like knowing their food is fresh.

feels. There's a bit of danger. Tentacles have sucking cups. They can grab the inside of throats. This can choke people.

chapter four

Rocky Mountain Oysters

"Rocky Mountain oysters" aren't oysters. They're a bull's private parts. They're peeled. They're dipped in flour. They're salted. They're peppered. They're pounded flat. Finally, they're deep-fried. They're served with cocktail sauce.

Rocky Mountain oysters are popular in the American West. They're also popular in western Canada. They're connected to cattle farming. Cattle farmers often remove the bulls' private parts. They do this to **tame** the animals. Tame means to train or control.

Rocky Mountain oysters can also come from bison, pigs, or sheep.

Cowboys ate these "oysters" a lot. They didn't waste any part of animals. This strange food was cheap. It was healthy.

chapter five

Fruit Bats

Some Asians eat fruit bats. Fruit bats are known as "chickens of the cave."

Fruit bat soup comes from Guam. People catch the bat. They rinse it off. They boil it. They add vegetables. They add coconut milk. Then, they eat it. They eat the fur. They eat the eyes. They eat the wings.

Eating this can be dangerous. Fruit bats eat plants. Some plants have poison. These poisons cause brain damage.

Some fruit bats may have full bellies.

Fruit bats smell like pee when cooked.

Their bodies could have poisons. People could eat these poisons. They could hurt their brains. Some people like the risk. They're extreme eaters!

chapter six

Hair

Some people pull out their hair. Then, they eat it. This can cause a **hairball**. Hairballs are balls of hair. They have "tails." The tails are hair trails. Hairballs collect in stomachs. This happens after about six months. People can get sick. They have stomach pain. They feel like throwing up. At least four people have died from having a hairball.

There was a girl. She lived in Chicago. She was 18 years old. She ate her hair. She had a 10-pound (4.5 kg) hairball in her stomach. Doctors removed it. This happened in 2007.

Eating your hair is called Rapunzel syndrome.

chapter seven

Rotten Birds

Kiviak is very strange! People say it is death stuffed in death. It's from Greenland.

Inuits are native people. They live in the Arctic areas. They make kiviak. They skin a seal. They remove the meat. They leave a thick layer of fat. They sew it into a bag. They stuff 500 auks in the seal bag. Auks are birds. They're stuffed whole. They still have beaks. They still have feet. They still have feathers. Auks rot inside. They rot for 7 months. Then it's ready to eat.

Kiviak has to be eaten outside. It's very smelly.

Kiviak looks like chunky meat soup. It's eaten raw. It's eaten in winter. It's served at parties. It tastes like cheese. The best part is auk hearts.

chapter eight

Pee

Some people drink pee. Some do this to survive. Some enjoy the taste. Some Middle Easterners taste camel pee. They're checking if the camel is pregnant.

Dongyang is a place in China. The people there eat special eggs. The eggs are called Virgin Boy Eggs. These people eat this in the spring. They collect pee from young boys. They get pee from school toilets. They soak eggs in the pee. They boil eggs in the pee. The shells crack. This lets flavor seep in. The eggs are boiled more. Cooking takes all day. The eggs are yellow.

These eggs are a traditional meal.

chapter nine

Poop

Some scientists are studying eating poop. They think it can help people lose weight. They study our guts. Our guts have germs. Some germs are good. Some germs are bad. Scientists made pills. They're poop pills. They contain good germs. They're taken from skinny people's poop.

Some people like poop in their coffee. Black ivory coffee is made from elephant poop. Thai elephants eat coffee beans.

 They digest the beans. They poop it out. People pick the beans out. They clean the beans. They roast the beans. They make coffee.

Black Ivory coffee beans have to be digested by an elephant.

25

Ken Shimizu lives in Japan. He owns a restaurant. He makes special curry. The curry tastes like poop. It looks like poop. It feels like poop. It smells like poop. It's served in a special bowl. The bowl looks like a toilet.

The curry doesn't have real poop in it. It has green tea. It has bitter melon. It has cocoa powder. It has onions and carrots. It has curry powder. It has kusaya. Kusaya is dried, rotten fish. It smells like dog poop.

Some people wonder what poop tastes like.

26

Spotlight Biography

Janice Poon styles food. She worked on a television show. It was about a man who eats humans! She made special food. The food looked like human parts. She needed to make a human leg. She tried to get giraffe meat. She called a few zoos. That didn't work. So, she got creative. She sewed different meats together. She put one kind of meat on a different bone. She sewed pork muscle over leg bones of a baby cow and lamb. She wrapped it with leaves. She decorated it. She used fruits and flowers. She said, "I want … the food to look so delicious that you want to reach into the screen and try it."

chapter ten

People

Cannibals eat human flesh. Eating humans is **taboo**. Taboo means not allowed. Some cannibals are extreme. They eat themselves. Marco Evaristti is an artist. He was born in Chile. He lives in Denmark. He had surgery. He got fat removed. He saved his fat. He ate it. He did this in 2007. He hosted a dinner. He made pasta. He made meatballs. He used ground beef. He added his fat. He served dinner. He shocked his friends. Someone asked how the meatballs tasted. He said, "Even better than my grandmother's."

Eating people can make people sick.

The most extreme cannibals eat dead humans. The Aghori monks live in India. They paint their faces white. They pray on top of dead bodies. They live in **graveyards**. Graveyards are places where dead bodies are buried.

They use what others throw away. They eat garbage. They eat rotten food. Some say they eat human flesh. They drink human pee. They eat human poop.

Some people get **cremated**. Cremate means to burn bodies. It makes ashes. The Aghori use these ashes. They spread them on their bodies.

The Aghori seek a greater power.

Try This!

- Make leftovers soup. Look in your fridge. Get food. Put it in a pot. Add water. Boil water. Add salt and pepper. Enjoy! (Rule: Don't buy any new food.)

- Eat something new. Be brave!

- Pick a color. Only eat foods of that color. Do this for one day.

- Talk to someone from a different culture. Ask what foods he or she eats. Eat something from that culture.

- Eat a bug! (Learn about the bug. Make sure it is safe to eat.)

- Keep a food journal. Write down everything you eat. Do this for one week. Count how many times you ate the same thing.

Consider This!

Take a Position! Reread the Table of Contents. How would you rank this list? Which food is the strangest? Which food is the least strange? Argue your point with reasons and evidence.

Say What? People eat many strange things. Research a strange food. Explain what it is. Explain why it is strange. Pretend that you're adding another chapter to this book.

Think About It! Food is part of our culture. Different cultures have different foods. What factors affect what people eat? What factors affect how people eat? What is considered to be American foods?

Learn More!

- Baines, Rebecca, ed. *Weird but True Food: 300 Bite-Sized Facts about Incredible Edibles*. Washington, DC: National Geographic, 2015.
- Eamer, Claire, and Sa Boothroyd (illustrator). *The World in Your Lunch Box: The Wacky History and Weird Science of Everyday Foods*. Toronto: Annick Press, 2012.
- Klepeis, Alicia Z. *The World's Strangest Foods*. North Mankato, MN: Capstone Press, 2015.
- Yerdon, Joe. *America's Oddest Foods*. New York: Gareth Stevens Publishing, 2016.

Glossary

cannibals (KAN-uh-buhlz) humans that eat other humans

cremated (KREE-mate-id) when a dead body is burned to ashes

expert (EK-spurt) a person who knows a lot about a topic

graveyards (GRAVE-yahrdz) places where dead bodies are buried

hairball (HAIR-bawl) a ball of hair that gets trapped in stomachs

kaolin (KAY-uh-lin) soft, white, chalky dirt

kusaya (koo-SI-yuh) Japanese salted dried fish that smells really bad

pregnant (PREG-nuhnt) carrying a baby

survive (sur-VIVE) to stay alive

taboo (tah-BOO) forbidden, not allowed

tame (TAYM) to train or control

tentacles (TEN-tuh-kuhlz) long arms, sometimes with sucking cups

Index